The Country Houses and Castles of R(

Volume Two: Upper Deeside

W. Stewart Wilson

Kincardine House

Kincardine House, now referred to as Kincardine Castle, overlooks Kincardine O' Neil, reckoned to be the oldest village in Deeside. It was built in 1894-96 for Mary and Frank Pickering. The architects were Niven and Wigglesworth of London and the builder was John Morgan. He had served his apprenticeship with his uncle Adam Mitchell whose business he took over after his death in 1877. The house and estate would normally have passed to their only son Francis, known as Frank, who had been wounded in the Boer War. At the outbreak of the Great War he rejoined his unit, the famous Scots Greys, and served in Flanders in 1914, in Gallipoli in 1915. On 23rd December 1917 he was killed at Passchendaele near Ypres leaving Kincardine with no male heir. Mary Pickering passed her estate over to Frank's older sister Ursula, the grandmother of the present owner. The house looks south and commands a spectacular view into the Dee Valley.

Text © W. Stewart Wilson, 2020.
First published in the United Kingdom, 2020,
Reprinted 2021,
by Stenlake Publishing Ltd.,
54-58 Mill Square,
Catrine, Ayrshire,
KA5 6RD

Telephone: 01290 551122
www.stenlake.co.uk

Printed by Blissetts,
Unit 1, Shield Drive,
West Cross Industrial Park,
Brentford, TW8 9EX

ISBN 9781840338553

**The publishers regret that they cannot supply
copies of any pictures featured in this book.**

Acknowledgements

I should like to thank all those who have given of their local knowledge including Gordon Casely, Chis Engel, Jim Henderson, Professor David Walker and David W. Walker.

Introduction

The Royal Burgh of Aberdeen lies between two rivers, the Dee and the Don. Joseph Robertson, the Scottish historian, writing in the 1843, compares the two but it is clear which he favours:

> *'A mile of Don's worth two of Dee*
> *Except for salmon, stone and tree'.*

Robertson then adds 'the Dee has the advantage of Don in its air, which is extremely fresh and pure (as particularly in Durris, Birse and Braemar) by means of its heath and woods; so it is observed that the people along it are very healthy and long-lived. Dr Alexander Fraser of Durris was wont to compare the air there with that of Windsor the finest in England.'

In 1847 Queen Victoria and Prince Albert had a miserable wet holiday at Ardverikie, Loch Laggan and her doctor, Sir James Clark, persuaded them to try the drier climate of Deeside. The Queen arrived at Aberdeen on Friday 8th September 1848 and as she drove up the Deeside road to view the Balmoral estate for the first time, her carriage passed under 23 triumphal arches. She quickly absorbed the spirit of relaxation in the Highland environment and as she remarked at the time – 'all seemed to breathe freedom and peace and to make us forget the world and its turmoils'. In June 1852 the old castle and estate of Balmoral was purchased by Prince Albert for a cost of £31,500 from the trustees of the Earl of Fife. Soon after the Queen received a £500,000 bequest in the will of the wealthy and eccentric John Camden Nield. In her diary for 1852 the Queen records 'a very handsome fortune had inexplicably been bequeathed to me'. This no doubt contributed to the decision to demolish the old castle and use the bequest to build the new Balmoral in its place. The new castle was built 100 yards north-west from the original one and considered to have a better vista. Balmoral is a private property and, unlike the monarch's official residences, is not the property of the Crown. On the death of Queen Victoria in 1901, the castle and estate passed, by the terms of her will, to Edward VII and succeeding British monarchs. Today it is the private home of the monarch.

Balmoral

Queen Victoria may have been the first British monarch to visit Deeside but the kings and queens of Scotland had found the pleasures and beauties in much earlier times. In the 8th century Angus, King of the Picts, built a timber fort near where Braemar Castle is today. Over 200 years elapsed before the next royal visitor; King Kenneth II came on a hunting trip and gave his name to the hill overlooking Braemar – Creag Choinnich in Gaelic or Craig Kenneth. Kings Malcolm II and Malcolm III were also frequent visitors. It is claimed that Malcolm III and his Queen in 1060 held a gathering and awarded prizes for strength and skill including a race up Creag Choinnich. Today much the same takes place each year on the 1st Saturday in September at the Braemar Gathering. In 1390 King Robert III granted a charter to his brother in law, Sir Malcolm Drummond, to erect a tower at Kindrochit on the east bank of the River Clunie. He never was to see the tower completed and was murdered by the Earl of Mar who finished the work. The castle, which was of immense strategic importance guarding routes from the south, is known to have been visited by Scottish kings until the 16th century. By the reign of James V it had fallen into disrepair and was certainly ruinous by 1618. So it remained until 1925 when under the auspices of The Deeside Field Club, Dr. W. Douglas Simpson began systematic excavation and surveyed the ruins.

The building of Balmoral marked an important point in the history of the valley. Deeside became very fashionable and it was a place for the wealthy to add to their property or build a fine country house, take part in the pleasure of fishing, hunting and of course to enjoy the rich countryside. But what about these new builds? Fenton Wyness suggests that 'visitors to Deeside might be surprised to find such a variety. Side by side with the native castellated keep towers and tower houses are to be seen buildings which might have been transported in toto from another part of the country or abroad'.

Two World Wars and the heavy burden of inheritance tax have left their mark. No longer is it possible to maintain great castles.

Kindrochit

This book shares the history of some of the many country houses and castles of Upper Deeside and is the companion volume to the one for Lower Deeside. Details of architecture can be explored in other books but especially:

Deeside and the Mearns – an illustrated Architectural Guide by Jane Geddes published in 2001.
Aberdeenshire: South and Aberdeen by Joseph Sharples, David Walker and Matthew Woodworth published in 2015.

Dess House

Dess House, originally known as Desswood, is a Baronial mansion built in 1851 by Thomas Mackenzie for an Aberdeen lawyer, Alexander Davidson. The addition in 1910 by their son Lt. Col. Duncan Davidson was undertaken by his brother Walter Ramsay Davidson. It consisted of an loggia with arches and columns and created a wonderful sheltered terrace to take full advantage of the grounds and the stunning countryside views. Walter had set up business as an architect in 1900 and on the death of his elder brother in 1928 he inherited Dess and retired from practice. The east wing was destroyed in a fire in 1956.

Tullochvenus

The present Tullochvenus is situated north of Lumphanan and dates from 1872 when it was rebuilt by William Ironside, a builder from Aberdeen. It replaced an earlier house on the site which belonged to Samuel Emslie (sometimes written Elmslie). He died in 1830 and was followed by his son James. In January 1843 a case for damages was brought by Francis Gordon Fraser of Findrach, whose estate included Tolmauds, lying to the east of Tullochvenus, to determine the boundary between the two properties. Fraser claimed it was the summit of Tulloch whereas Emslie claimed it to be further to the east on Findrach owned land. It would appear that the court did not come to any conclusion, having already considered the dispute some years previously. James Emslie died in 1870 and thereafter the house had many owners. In the 1920s and 1930s Lydia Mary Ireland lived here. Although she moved to Pennsylvania when she was in her 80s she retained fond memories of her days in the house and her last will begins 'I Lydia M. Ireland of Lumphanan, Aberdeenshire Scotland'. When she lived in Tullochvenus, her son, Harold Ireland, had a silver fox farm nearby which closed in the 1940s.

Camphill House

The estate of Camphill, which in 1783 belonged to Sir William Forbes of Craigievar, was bought by Joseph Emslie, born prior to 1770. Andrew Jervise, in his book *Epitaphs and Inscriptions*, published in 1879, comments that Joseph 'made money as a merchant in Tarland and bought the estate of Camphill in Lumphanan'. In the *Aberdeenshire: South and Aberdeen Architectural Guide* the authors describe the original house as having 'a two storey front, three windows wide in pink ashlar granite with gabled roof and coped stacks, dated 1827 at its skews'. Emslie and his wife Jean Leslie, had four of a family, two sons and two daughters. Two died young, a son James in 1818, aged three, and a daughter, Ann in 1823, aged 15. Joseph died in 1849 aged 82 and his wife in 1851, aged 72. The surviving son Alexander had died in 1850 at the early age of 40. The surviving daughter Margaret married a relation, James Emslie of Tullochvenus and died in 1874, aged 58. A relation of the family Jean Emslie and widow of Rev. John Aulay Maclennan, came to live there until her death in 1882, aged 63. A much later addition to the house was the single storey with attic windows added to the right.

Auchenhove

Just over a mile south-west of Lumphanan is Auchenhove and nearby the site of the Loch of Auchlossan. In 1859 the proprietors of the adjoining lands – the Marquis of Huntly and Farquharson of Finzean, who at that time was the landlord of Auchenhove, formed a scheme to drain it and so provide additional land for cultivation. James W. Barclay, afterwards MP for Forfarshire and his brother, who were seedsmen and agricultural suppliers, undertook the work. When the Barclays gave up their interest in the farm of Mains of Auchlossan, the reclaimed land was divided between that farm and East Mains of Auchenhove. It was soon thereafter that the loch started re-appearing and taking back control of a large acreage. It was not until the Second World War that the government stepped in to once again reclaim the land as part of the war effort. Today the land has dried up again but for how long is hard to forecast. The present Auchenhove House dates from the 19th century and was originally built as a dower house for the laird of Finzean. The lands of Auchenhove were sold in 1888 when they were purchased by Charles Stephen Leslie. Since that time there have been several changes of ownership.

Findrach

The village of Lumphanan is of ancient origin and derives its name from the Welsh *llan* a 'church' or 'enclosure' and Finan, the Welsh missionary and disciple of St. Mungo who brought Christianity to these parts in the 7th century. The tradition of Macbeth pervades the area – his death took place within the bounds of the parish of Lumphanan and not as related by Shakespeare at Dunsinane. Findrach House has its origins as an 18th century farmhouse. In 1670 Frances Fraser purchased Findrach estate from Sir Robert Forbes of Learney and it remained in the Fraser family for the next 200 years. It was extended into a two storey country house by architect William Smith in 1862. Since that date the house has seen many additions. Of especial merit is the walled garden restored to its former glory by the current owner. In 2019 planning permission was granted for demolition of Findrach and replacement by a new house on the site.

Glenmillan House

Glenmillan House, near Lumphanan, was built for Robert Smith of Smith and Cochran, Aberdeen advocates, by the architect James Matthews in 1872. The house incorporated features from an earlier house. Matthews had been a Aberdeen city councillor from 1863-71 but recalled in 1883 to be Lord Provost. He was responsible for implementing the Aberdeen City Improvement Act of 1883 which included building Schoolhill and Rosemount Viaduct, giving improved access to the city. The east wing of the house was lost in a fire in the 1940s. Still to be seen is an interesting tympanum, a decorative semicircular arch, dated 1688, above the entrance to the stables.

Corse Castle and Corse House

This ruinous Corse Castle built for William Forbes in 1581 is situated about three miles north from Lumphanan. It replaced an earlier house which had been destroyed by brigands. The Corse Burn, which runs through the hollow was dammed up, forming a fine sheet of water to the south of the castle. The castle became redundant in the mid-19th century, and was replaced in 1863 by a new house for James Ochonar Forbes. Alexander Ellis was the architect and his use of the square Italian style belvedere tower at the centre of the villa shows the influence of Alexander 'Greek' Thomson, the famous Scottish architect. The gardens were originally laid out by the artist James Giles.

HOUSE OF CROMAR, TARLAND.   J.J.B.

THE ITALIAN GARDENS, ALASTREAN HOUSE, TARLAND

House of Cromar / Alastrean House

The 7th Earl of Aberdeen's family home was at Haddo but he also owned the Cromar estate. On one of his visits with his wife to Cromar she fell in love with the countryside and persuaded him to build a house, completed in 1905, which they called House of Cromar. The Earl became a Marquis in 1916 and four years later he reached an agreement with Alexander, later Sir Alexander MacRobert, under the terms of which the house and estate of Cromar would pass to him, or his heirs, on his death. Sir Alexander predeceased him but when the Marquis died in 1934, Lady MacRobert inherited the estate. She continued to live in Douneside and only used House of Cromar for special occasions. In 1943 she renamed the house Alastrean House, meaning 'Hearth of Honour for Winged Heroes of the Stars'. The house was placed at the disposal of the Royal Air Force and Commonwealth Air Force, as a rest centre for operational crew. It continued to be used as such after the war, but in 1952 was damaged by fire. It was rebuilt and re-opened again in 1958. In 1984 the MacRobert Trustees offered the use of Alastrean House to the RAF Benevolent Fund as a retirement home and it continued in this role, with two new wings added, until 2005. The trustees then leased the house to the Balhousie Care Group who use it as a residential care home with respite facilities.

Douneside

Alexander McRobert (sic), born in Aberdeen in 1854, was a self-made millionaire who came from a working-class background. He left school when he was twelve to start his working life but by attending evening classes he gained several qualifications. In 1884 Mac, as he became known, travelled to India to take up employment in a woollen mill and later was appointed the manager of Cawnpore Woollen Mills. He bought the small house and farm of Burnside in 1888 as a home for his ageing parents. The farm was renamed Douneside and when his parents died in the early 1900s he turned the house into a small country mansion and added a tower and later the two wings. His first wife had died while he was in India and Rachel, who he married in 1911, developed the splendid gardens which are still a feature today. They were blessed with three sons, Alasdair, Roderic and Iain. Alexander was knighted in 1910 and in 1922 he received his baronetcy and created first Baronet of Cawnpore and Cromar. It was only then that he changed his surname from McRobert to MacRobert. Sir Robert died later that year but further family tragedy was to follow. In 1938 Alasdair was killed in a flying accident and his two brothers lost their lives in 1941 while serving in the Royal Air Force. Lady MacRobert donated £25,000 to the nation to purchase a Stirling bomber which she asked to be named 'MacRobert's Reply'. Two years later she set up the MacRobert Trust which continues to award grants to all sections of both the local and a much wider community. The historic house re-opened its doors after a major renovation on 1st June 2016, offering guests a luxurious Scottish countryside stay.

Corrachree House

Corrachree House, near Tarland, was built in 1842 by James Henderson, an Aberdeen architect, for Major John Farquharson of the East India Company. Though lying on the edge of Tarland village, Corrachree falls within Logie Coldstone parish. Colonel Sir John Farquharson was born in 1839 John Cosmo MacPherson, the son of Charles MacPherson, minister of Tomintoul, and Mary Farquharson. He took the name Farquharson after inheriting Corrachree (also known as Logie-Mar) in 1871 from his mother's brother John Farquharson. In 1880 the new owner made additions to the house included the balustrade portico. He had attended Marischal College in Aberdeen and the Royal Military College, Woolwich before being commissioned in the Royal Engineers. He joined the Ordnance Survey in 1872, and was appointed director-general in 1894, in which capacity he served until his retirement in 1899.

Tillypronie House

Tillypronie House, situated to the north of Logie Coldstone, was built by Sir John Clark, son of Sir James Clark, physician to Queen Victoria. He had purchased Pronie estate in 1855 and at first the family stayed in the old farmhouse of Pronie until the new Tillypronie House was built in 1867. Tillypronie was frequently visited by Queen Victoria, who was usually accompanied by her faithful servant, John Brown. It is said that he considered himself too grand to dine with the Clarks' domestic staff and a special hut was built outside the front door of the house to which his meals were taken. The American author Henry James, on a visit in 1878, wrote that 'this supremely comfortable house – lying deep among the brown and purple moors – has the honour, I believe, of being the highest placed laird's house in Scotland.' Sir Thomas Royden, Chairman of Cunard, purchased the house in 1925 and made many improvements to it and the gardens. It is claimed that in 1934 it was Thomas, by then Lord Royden, who asked King George V if he would approve the naming of the new ship after 'England's greatest Queen', meaning Queen Victoria, to which the King replied 'My wife would be honoured and delighted'. Hence the ship was named *Queen Mary*. During the Second World War, the house was home to the boarders of the kindergarten and lower school of Albyn School for Girls who had moved from Aberdeen for safety. In 1951 Gavin Astor purchased the whole estate and the present owner is his son the Hon. Philip Astor.

Blelack House

Blelack House, a Scottish mansion house near the village of Logie Coldstone, has its origins in the 17th century. The estate belonged to a branch of the powerful Clan Gordon. Two dates are engraved on the façade of the building, 1881 and 1892. There is good evidence that the house is older, these being renovation dates. Blelack House was burnt to the ground in retribution after the young laird, Charles Gordon had joined the 1745 Jacobite rising. He finally had the forfeited lands of Blelack restored to him in 1784 and set about rebuilding the house before his death the following year. The estate was sold by his grandson in 1794 to William Gordon, no relative of the original Gordon family. In 1862 Sir Alexander Anderson, Lord Provost of Aberdeen, bought the house and three years later Sir Thomas Coltman acquired the estate for his son William. The house was accidently destroyed by fire in 1868 but it was rebuilt and then used as a hunting lodge. During the Second World War senior pupils from Albyn School for Girls in Aberdeen were evacuated there. The building was split up into separate flats in 1976.

Aboyne Castle

The lands of Aboyne passed through many families until the mid 14th century when they were held by William Keith, Great Marischal of Scotland. In 1408 Alexander Seton married Elizabeth Gordon, the daughter of Adam de Gordon, Lord of Gordon and Elizabeth Keith, daughter of William Keith the then Marischal of Scotland. On the death of her parents Alexander Seton inherited the lands and changed his name to Alexander Gordon. In 1449 he was created 1st Earl of Huntly. In 1599 the 6th Earl of Huntly became Marquis of Huntly. It was not until after 1660 when Charles Gordon, the fourth son of the 2nd Marquis, had been created 1st Earl of Aboyne that the first tower house was built. In 1888 Sir William Cunliffe Brooks acquired Aboyne Castle from his son-in-law the 11th Marquis who was heavily in debt. George Truefitt, the architect, continued with the improvements he had started but these were not completed before Brooks' death in 1900. The castle was then sold and it was recovered by the family in the 1970s by the 13th Marquis and 9th Earl of Aboyne. In recent years these Victorian additions have been demolished and some of the stonework used to restore the remaining tower house in 17th century Scottish castellated style.

Birse Lodge

Birse Lodge, built in 1861 of rough-faced pink granite, faces south across Charlestown Road towards the River Dee. It was originally called Huntly Lodge and served as the dower house for the Huntly Marchionesses from Aboyne Castle, and formed part of the castle policies. On an estate a dower house was usually a moderately large house available for use by the widow of the previous owner of the estate. The widow, often known as the dowager, usually moved into the dower house from the larger family house on the death of her husband allowing the new heir to occupy the now vacated principal house. In the early 1990s the house became a hotel.

Glentanar & the Tower of Ess

On the South Deeside road and heading west from Aboyne is the Tower of Ess and a road leading into the Glentanar Estate. Glen Tanar House was built by George Truefitt on the site of a small 17th century farmhouse called Woodend, for William Cunliffe Brooks, later Sir William, a wealthy Manchester banker who had arrived in 1869 at Glen Tanar (also spelt Tanner or Tana). At the time of construction, he was a tenant of Charles Gordon, 11th Marquis of Huntly, who had married his daughter. He purchased the estate in 1874 which had been put up for sale to pay for the Gordon family debts. Fenton Wyness, the noted historian and architect, in his book *Royal Valley*, did not approve of the style of house 'it is clear that he failed to appreciate that Scotland possessed any architectural tradition for he immediately set about eliminating everything which appeared incongruous to his English eyes'. On his death the estate was bought in 1905 by George Coats of the cotton firm of Paisley who was created 1st Baron Glentanar in 1916. The house was demolished in 1975 and rebuilt for the Hon. Jean Bruce, grand-daughter of the first baron.

Craigendinnie

Sir William Cunliffe Brooks of Glen Tana (his preferred spelling), died in 1900 and it had been his wish that his eldest grandson Ean Cecil on reaching his 25th birthday should continue to occupy and manage his estate. He was the son of Edith, Sir William's daughter. and was born in 1880. In the meantime the estate was leased to Mr. George Coats, the owner of the cotton firm in Paisley. This resulted in both Lady Brooks being without a home, and she built for herself a house called The Neuk, while Edith, Lady Francis Cecil, whose husband had predeceased her, lived in Craigendinnie, a house on the estate

The Neuk

on the south side of the Dee. The house had been built in 1894 by architect George Truefitt and in 1929 it was extended and altered by the architect George Bennett Mitchell. Sir William's wish that Ean Cecil should take over the mantle of laird did not materialise and in 1905 Glen Tana was sold to George Coats, later Lord Glentanar. Aboyne Castle estate was retained and not sold until 1923 when it was acquired by James Mearns, a successful Aberdeen businessman. Ean Cecil, a generous benefactor to Aboyne and especially to the golf club, died at Fasnadaroch in 1942.

Struan Hall

Struan Hall is described as 'a beautiful home, quietly situated in the village of Aboyne, on Royal Deeside'. The house was originally situated some five miles to the east of Aboyne where it was known as Tillydrine House. In 1904 it was moved stone by stone to its present location. It is a substantial villa and retains numerous details of interest, including pyramidal roofed entrance tower, decorative ironwork, and patterned timber balcony and fencing. It is now a popular bed and breakfast establishment.

Dinnet House

Alexander Marshall Mackenzie of Aberdeen was the architect of Dinnet House, built in 1890 for Charles Wilson. The house of grey granite and of three storeys served as a somewhat grand shooting lodge for Charles Wilson who was a prominent English ship owner. He also served as Liberal MP for Hull for 30 years, and in 1906 received the title Baron Nunburnholme. In 1896 the house and estate was sold to James Charles Barclay-Harvey. In 1905 the house suffered a fire which destroyed the two upper floors, but the original architect restored the house and added a square entrance tower. On the death of his father in 1924 it became the home of Sir Charles Malcolm Barclay-Harvey, who served as MP for Kincardine and Aberdeenshire West from 1923 to 1929 and from 1931 to 1939 and was knighted in the King's Birthday Honours in 1936, for his political and public services. He served as Governor of South Australia from 1939 until 1944. On his return to his estate he became renowned for his land management until his death in 1969. The house and estate is still owned by the family.

Fasnadarroch House

George Truefitt's next major design for William Cunliffe Brooks was Fasnadarroch House, a fishing lodge on the South Deeside road west of the entrance to Glen Tana (Cunliffe Brook's preferred spelling). It was built in 1874, the year of his daughter Edith's marriage to Francis Cecil, and may have been a wedding present to the pair, though he retained ownership. Lord Francis Cecil was the second son of the Marquis of Exeter. Cecil pursued a career in the Royal Navy and in 1877 he was made a partner in Cunliffe, Brooks & Co but it did not work out for him. His Navy career had given him an addiction for sailing and he spent what his father had settled on him at marriage on buying a 40-ton racing cutter. He depended on his wife, Edith, to pay for the upkeep of Stocken Hall, the rented house they had in England, from the marriage settlement from her father. In 1889 Lord Cecil was declared bankrupt and death followed that year. William Cunliffe Brooks died in 1900 and under his will Fasnadarroch passed into the ownership of Edith, Lady Francis Cecil. The house had originally been a very simple fishing lodge but she had it extended for her use in 1901.

Glenmuick House

House of Glenmuick was built in 1871-73 for Sir James Mackenzie who in 1838 had gone out to an indigo plantation in India where he made a very substantial fortune. Sir James was a friend of the Prince of Wales, later King Edward VII, who became a regular guest at the house. The house was ideally situated with great stalking opportunities and also excellent grouse moors. One of his many guests was less than complimentary about the house, suggesting that its situation 'was selected with the view to impress the good people of Ballater rather with the importance of its owner, than to provide a comfortable house for himself and his guests'. In 1889 the house played host to the Shah of Persia who was on a visit to Britain. He used House of Glenmuick rather than stay at Balmoral as guest of Queen Victoria. In 1890 James was created Sir James Mackenzie, of Glenmuick 1st Baronet but he died less than five months later. The house was demolished in 1948 and the name was transferred to the former Brackley House which had been the dower house to the old house.

Brackley House

Brackley was built for Sir Allan Mackenzie, James Mackenzie's eldest son, on the site of the old Brackley Castle and was enlarged from a small farmhouse first in 1895 with an additional wing added in 1912.

Knock Castle

Knock Castle was granted in 1562 to the Gordons of Abergeldie by the 4th Earl of Huntly, as a reward for their support at the Battle of Corrichie. A feud between the neighbouring clan, the Forbeses of Strathgirnock, intensified when Henry Gordon 2nd laird of Knock, was murdered in 1592 during a raid by the Forbes men. His brother, Alexander Gordon, succeeded Henry, and may have built the castle in 1600. There is a horrifying story attached to the family. One day when Alexander's seven sons were out cutting peat they strayed onto the Forbes lands where they were set upon. After a fierce battle, all the brothers were killed by the Forbes men and their severed heads impaled on their peat spades. The laird was concerned that the boys had not returned and sent his servant out to look for them. When he discovered the boy's heads, he ran back to tell the laird what had happened. Upon hearing the news, Alexander Gordon collapsed at the top of the castle's turnpike stair and fell to his death. The Forbes laird was then taken and executed and all his lands forfeited to Abergeldie. Knock Castle is now a ruin and under the protection of Historic Environment Scotland.

Birkhall

The Gordons of Abergeldie acquired the estate from the Farquharson family in the year 1715. Prince Albert purchased Birkhall in 1849 for the Prince Edward, later King Edward VII. In 1856 Florence Nightingale, tired and ill after the privations of the Crimean War, was invited to come for some respite. While there, and encouraged by Queen Victoria, she planned her strategy to improve the Army medical service. It was in the garden of Birkhall that the Secretary of State for War, Lord Panmure, agreed to the setting up of the Royal Army Medical Corps. Prince Edward only used Birkhall once in 1862, preferring Abergeldie Castle and so in 1885 he sold it to his mother, Queen Victoria. In the 1930s it was used by the Duke and Duchess of York, later King George VI and Queen Elizabeth, who holidayed there with their children, Princess Elizabeth and Princess Margaret. The house was redecorated by the Yorks who also replanted the gardens. After the death of King George VI, it became the holiday home of the Queen Mother who added substantially to the house. Since 2002, Prince Charles, Duke of Rothesay is regularly in residence at Birkhall.

Abergeldie Castle

Abergeldie Castle lies six miles from Ballater on the south bank of the Dee, and the estate adjoins that of Balmoral. The original building, a Gordon castle dating from the 16th century, was a plain, square turreted tower but it was gutted by fire in 1816 and rebuilt with an altered roofline. By 1832 the *Aberdeen Journal* reported that 'it was ready for rent'. The estate was leased in 1848 by Prince Albert and considerable additions were made to make it more comfortable for the reception of guests. It was frequently occupied by the Duchess of Kent, Queen Victoria's mother, until she died in 1861 and thereafter was used by the Prince of Wales, the future King Edward VII, and his family. The additions made by Prince Albert were removed in 1970 when the castle was returned to the Gordon family. In the storms of January 2016 part of the embankment was washed away and the castle was in danger of being swallowed up by the swollen River Dee. The castle has been saved but the suspension footbridge which linked the castle with the north bank of the Dee built in 1885 was washed away.

Cambus O' May House

The *Aberdeen Journal* of 19th September 1874 reports that 'here, on the hill, or some distance up, the architect, George Truefitt, is putting up a capital house for Mr. H. L Gaskell, – dining room, drawing room, library, billiard-room, and lots of bedrooms. There will be three gables in front, towards the road, the centre one stepped, and below it a large bay window and verandah around it'. Henry Lomax Gaskell had married Alice, the sister of Sir William Cunliffe Brooks. She died aged only 50 in 1872. Cambus O' May house was used as a fishing lodge and was ideally situated overlooking the Dee and close to the railway station. Beyond the station is a suspension bridge of 1905 which was rebuilt in 1988 but badly damaged in the storms of December 2015.

THE LILY POND, CAMBUS O' MAY HOTEL.

Tullich Lodge

Shortly before reaching Ballater is Tullich Lodge, perched high on the hill with a commanding view of the plain below. The house was built in 1897 as a hunting lodge for an Aberdeen advocate, William Reid. The architect was Alexander Marshall Mackenzie and the tower was added in 1910 with further additions in 1923. The architect for these additions was E. Vincent Harris. Later it became a hotel but it is now back to being a private house. The house overlooks the old Tullich Kirk. In the 1200s, Tullich Kirk was granted by David I to the Knights Templar. Although abandoned as a place of worship in 1798, Tullich Kirk and the circular kirkyard that surrounds it was never abandoned as a place of burial. The story is told how on one wintry Sunday morning the minister was very late for the service and the congregation took to keeping themselves warm by dancing a reel in the kirkyard; hence *The Reel o Tullich*.

Monaltrie House

Monaltrie House was built by James Robertson in 1682 for Francis Farquharson of Monaltrie, known as Baron Ban because of his handsome looks and fair hair. He joined the Jacobite cause and following the Battle of Culloden in 1746, he was sent to the Tower of London. Although reprieved he was not pardoned and it was 20 years later before he was able to return to find his old home at Crathie burnt to the ground. He is attributed with setting out plans for the foundation of Ballater. He had discovered the medicinal properties at Pannanich Wells and built the inn for the people who flocked to the area to test the waters for themselves. Soon the accommodation could not cope with the influx and thus it was that nearby Ballater was developed by his nephew and successor William Farquharson. Before his death in 1790, Francis had been instrumental in the construction in 1783 of the first bridge across the Dee at Ballater. Monaltrie House was almost derelict by the 1970s but has now been extensively refurbished.

Oakhall

Oakhall has a commanding position overlooking Braemar Road and the Dee and contains many Baronial features, including what has been termed 'a castellated *sitooterie* on a castellated tower'. It is situated in an area of Ballater which underwent transformation from wooded countryside to an elite suburb during the last 30 years of the 19th century. Prestigious houses were built on spacious plots along the road, reflecting Ballater's popularity with the wealthy as a summer base to explore the surrounding countryside. This popularity was due in part to the proximity of Balmoral and the strong connections of the area with Queen Victoria. This house was built in 1890 for Dr. Alexander Ogilvie, headmaster of Robert Gordon's College in Aberdeen. It became a children's hotel in the 1940s and was later used as an annexe to Darroch Learg Hotel, originally a private house dating from 1888.

Craigendarroch House

In 1886 Charles Gordon, the 11th Marquis of Huntly, whose family had held the lands for centuries, sold some 10,000 acres to John Mitchell Keiller of Dundee. He was a descendant of Janet Keiller who along with her husband John had created their version of orange marmalade. The Keillers had come to enjoy holidays in Ballater, originally staying at Morven Lodge but requiring a more spacious home of their own built the house on the 'hill of the oaks' known in Gaelic as Craigendarroch. Rather than building with local granite, red sandstone was used brought all the way by rail from the Pentland Hills near Edinburgh. John Keiller died in 1899 leaving his son, Alexander then aged nine as heir, to the family fortune. During the Second World War the house was home to evacuees from Glasgow and army officers posted to Ballater for training exercises in the surrounding hills. At the end of the war the Keiller family sold the house which became a hotel, and later time-share apartments were built surrounding the original house.

Darroch Learg

Darroch Learg was built for Dr. Alexander Hendry in 1888. He was the son of a shopkeeper in Braemar who went on to study in Edinburgh for his medical degree. He returned to Deeside and served as a doctor for Ballater and Upper Deeside. When the First World War was declared, despite being the only doctor who had not left on war service, he too registered on condition that his own work was covered if he should be called away from Deeside. He served as surgeon apothecary to the royal household at Balmoral. In 1931 the lad, brought up above the Braemar shop, became Sir Alexander Hendry, Knight Commander of the Victorian Order, the personal gift of the then monarch King George V. This charming grey granite house later became a hotel ideally perched on the lower slope of Craigendarroch. Darroch Learg translates as 'the oak copse on the sunny hillside'. It suffered a major fire in 2015 but is now restored to its former glory.

Craigard House

Craigard House in Ballater, possibly dates from the early 20th century and is situated in the shadow of Craigendarroch. It commands wonderful views of the Dee Valley captured in the message written on the reverse of the card sent by a guest in March 1940 after it had become a hotel. 'We have a lovely view over the golf course to the hills with Lochnagar in the background'. Viewed from Ballater in the summer, the northern face of the moutain is often in shadow and takes on a brooding or, in Byron's poem, 'dark' appearance. He spent some time on Deeside during the summers of 1795-97, returning in 1803 when he climbed Lochnagar. Later in life he wrote in expressive terms about the mountain.

England! thy beauties are tame and domestic
To one who has roved o'er the mountains afar;
Oh for the crags that are wild and majestic!
The steep frowning glories of dark Lochnagar

Gairnshiel Lodge

Situated just outside Ballater, Gairnshiel Lodge, on the banks of the River Gairn, was a former hunting lodge used by Queen Victoria. The original lodge was built in 1746 with further extensions thereafter. Other members of the Royal Family who have used the lodge for hunting include King George V and King George VI. The lodge is now a hotel but it is said to be haunted. There have been sightings, so it is claimed, of the spirit of an old woman, who is thought to be a former owner of the lodge. Also the noise of marching men and the moving of horses and carts has been heard outside the lodge, though nothing can be seen. Perhaps it is the ghosts of the soldiers on the old General Wade military road which passes by. The road and the arched bridge was completed in 1749 and was built following the major unrest of Jacobite attacks and the Battle of Culloden.

THE ENTRANCE GATE BALMORAL CASTLE

E 03211

Balmoral Castle

Guarding the entrance to Balmoral. The gates were added in 1925 by King George V and Queen Mary. They were made by the Balmoral blacksmith and bear the monograms of the King and Queen. When Queen Victoria and Prince Albert bought Balmoral, the South Deeside Road continued through Balmoral to meet with the North Deeside Road at the Old Bridge of Dee at Invercauld, some three miles east of Braemar. To allow greater privacy, the road through Balmoral was closed and Prince Albert commissioned new bridges, suitable for wheeled traffic, to be built across the Dee at Crathie in 1857 to the design of Isambard Kingdom Brunel, and two years later at Invercauld.

Balmoral Castle (from the south)

In early times the lands of Balmoral formed part of the earldom of Mar. The original castle was built in the 15th century and consisted of a square tower with battlements. By 1746 a house had been added to it by the Farquarsons of Inverey. When Sir Robert Gordon, a younger brother of the 4th Earl of Aberdeen, acquired the lease in 1830 he demolished most of the building. He employed John Smith, Aberdeen city architect, to design a small castle with a mixture of Tudor and Scottish Baronial style. Sir Robert died in 1847 whereupon his lease on Balmoral reverted to his brother. In February 1848 Prince Albert acquired the remaining part of the lease, without having seen the property first! In September 1848 Queen Victoria arrived on Deeside with her family. The decision was taken in 1852 to buy the estate from James Duff, 5th Earl of Fife. The old castle was demolished and the present Balmoral built in its place, to the design of William Smith, who had succeeded his father as Aberdeen city architect. The foundation stone was laid in 1853, and it was completed in 1855.

Balmoral Castle, West Front.

Balmoral Castle (from the west)

The view is of the west front of the castle with Royal apartments on the first floor. Each morning at nine o'clock the Royal piper must play for 15 minutes under the monarch's window. The role was created by Queen Victoria after she discovered the Marquis of Breadalbane had his own piper. In a letter to her mother she wrote, 'we have heard nothing but bagpipes since we have been in the beautiful Highlands and I have become so fond of it that I mean to have a piper, who can if you like it, pipe every night at Frogmore'. The Royal apartments look out to formal gardens, to a design approved by Prince Albert. By 1876 the *Gardeners' Chronicle* recorded 'the upper flower garden slopes down toward the west and in the centre of the two grass terraces is a full-sized bronze wild boar, placed, as it were, sitting on its haunches, with its head and shoulders visible above the foliage, which has a strange but telling effect'. The deer statues were also located in this garden by then. The Royal Archive records that in June 1929 the stags and boar sited to the west of the castle were painted. These have since gone from the west garden, but one statue of a wild boar remains and is now placed to the south of the castle.

Balmoral Castle Ballroom

Balmoral Castle ballroom is the only part of the castle open to the public. It is probably most famously known as the setting for the annual Ghillies Ball, a tradition started by Queen Victoria in 1852 when she wanted to thank her servants and other members of her staff for their good service. The ball is a much anticipated event for everyone at Balmoral because of the opportunity for the servants to socialize and even dance with the Queen and her family. At first the ball was held in a temporary pre-fabricated iron building, ordered by Prince Albert, which was in use by October 1851. The present ballroom was completed in 1856 and still has many of the original features. The windows on the west wall were 'festooned with tartan curtains' and facing on the east wall the Royal alcove fitted with mirrors to reflect the light which gives the room a 'jewel like quality'. Across the north wall is a balustraded timber balcony used by the musicians at the ball.

Balmoral Castle (Garden Cottage)

The original Garden Cottage was a wooden building completed in 1863 and used by one of the Queen's gardeners. Two of the rooms were set aside for Queen Victoria who used them for taking breakfast, dealing with state correspondence and writing her diaries. It is recorded that in 1864, her lady-in-waiting, who had contracted scarlet fever, was isolated there until she recovered. Alterations and additions were made to the property but by 1894 the wooden cottage had fallen into disrepair and was demolished. The present cottage was completed in 1895 and was clad, in part, with Ballochbuie wood from the forest at the west end of the estate. The purchase of Ballochbuie in 1878 is commemorated by a cairn with the wording the 'Bonniest Plaid in Scotland' recalling the old legend that MacGregor, the last laird of Ballochbuie, sold the forest to Farquharson of Invercauld for a tartan plaid.

Allt-na-giubhsaich

Queen Victoria and Prince Albert's first visit to Balmoral was in 1848. It was during that holiday that they visited the hunting lodge called Allt-na-giubhsaich at the head of Loch Muick. In August of the following year they stayed overnight at this lodge which had been extended and improved although Victoria still regarded it as our 'little bothie'. Writing about its location she wrote that 'the scenery is beautiful here, so wild and grand – real severe Highland scenery, with trees in the hollow'.

Glas-allt-Shiel

In 1852 in the Queen's diary she describes pony riding and walking from Allt-na-giubhsaich to 500 feet above the loch and then descending Glas Allt past the 150-foot waterfall and stopping at Glas-allt-Shiel for a packed lunch in a 'charming room with a most lovely view'. This small cottage was at the time occupied by one of the Queen's keepers. After the death of Prince Albert the Queen could no longer bear to stay at Allt-na-giubhsaich with its associations and instead the cottage at Glas-allt-Shiel was extended and became her new retreat. It became known as the Widow's House or the Widow's Hut.

Invercauld House

The area was part of the ancient earldom of Mar. In a contract of August 1632 in which the Earl of Mar agreed to sell the lands of Invercauld to John Farquharson there is no mention of a house. His grandson Robert died in 1666 and by this time Invercauld House was a well-established property. Robert was followed by his brother Alexander, who commissioned the extensions of 1679. John Farquharson of Invercauld fought for the Jacobites and was taken prisoner at the Battle of Preston in 1715. Having been condemned to death and reprieved, he declined to rise in 1745, and as the result his estates were targeted and the house plundered, the laird himself having fled the area. The history of the house thereafter is very much of a family home. In the 1920s the estate flourished with excellent shooting and deer stalking and record grouse bags being taken. Today the estate is run as a modern business owned by family trusts under the guidance of Captain Farquharson of Invercauld and other members of his family.

Braemar Castle

Braemar Castle was built in 1628 as a hunting lodge by John Erskine, Earl of Mar as a bulwark against the rising power of the Farquharsons, but in 1689 it was burnt by the Black Colonel, John Farquharson of Inverey, to prevent it being used as garrison for the troops of General Mackay, a supporter of William of Orange. A later Earl of Mar acted as Secretary of State for Scotland and played a key role in the Act of Union between Scotland and England in 1707 but was stripped of his office on the accession of the Hanoverian King George I. It was then that he returned to his Deeside estates and called the disaffected Scottish chiefs to him at the Farquharson house of Invercauld, a mile from Braemar Castle which led him raising the standard for the Jacobite cause in the 1715 rising. His frequent changes of sides led to him being known as Bobbin Jock. Because of the part that he played in the Jacobite rising his estates and lands were forfeited to the crown. In 1732 Braemar Castle and estate was sold to the Farquharsons of Invercauld but the castle was in ruins. In 1748, three years after the second Jacobite rising, it was leased to the government as a garrison for Hanoverian troops and rebuilding started. It was not until 1797 that it was returned to the Farquharsons of Invercauld who made it into a family home. Since 2007 the castle has been leased to the local community and is now open as a museum.

Kindrochit Castle

In 1390 King Robert III granted a charter to his brother-in-law, Sir Malcolm Drummond, to erect a tower at Kindrochit on the east bank of the River Clunie. He never was to see the tower completed and was murdered by the Earl of Mar who finished the work. It was reported abandoned by 1618. A local legend tells the gruesome story that the castle was allowed to decay after an outbreak of the plague. According to the tale, when the castle inhabitants were struck down with the deadly illness, the castle was ordered to be destroyed trapping those inside thus preventing the plague from spreading. So the ruin remained until 1925 when under the auspices of The Deeside Field Club, Dr. W. Douglas Simpson and a group of Aberdeen Boy Scouts began systematic excavation of the site. The Kindrochit brooch, a late 15th-century silver-gilt Highland brooch, was discovered in the pit-prison of Kindrochit. The brooch was inscribed with the phrase 'I am in place of a friend'. The brooch is now at the National Museum of Scotland in Edinburgh. In the last few years, the castle has been rescued from decay by the local council, who spent £21,000 to stabilise the walls, clear the undergrowth and create pathways through the site.

Stair Kindrochit Castle Ruins, Braemar. M. 339.

Mar Lodge

About six miles west of Braemar the road reaches Victoria Bridge, a private bridge leading to Mar Lodge. This was not, however, the first Mar Lodge. The first was sited behind the present building and in the 18th century it was bought by the Earl of Fife. In the middle of the following century the family built a new mansion on the south side of the Dee which they first called Corriemulzie Cottage and later New Mar Lodge which was lost in a fire in 1895. That had been the home of the sixth Earl of Fife, later created Duke of Fife, who in 1889 had married Princess Louise, eldest daughter of the future King Edward VII. Queen Victoria laid the foundation stone of their new home in 1895 and the building was completed in 1898. Mar Lodge was extensively damaged by a fire while being renovated in 1991, but was rebuilt. It was converted into holiday flats and retains many of the features of its days as a hunting lodge. Mar Lodge Estate became a National Trust for Scotland property in 1995.